MW00891324

Exploring Ecosystems!

An Environmentally Friendly Coloring Book

Michael Dutton

Dover Publications, Inc.
Mineola, New York

Note

The Earth is a vast ecosystem (ecological system) of both living and nonliving things. But smaller ecosystems exist as well, such as a puddle, a pond, a lake, or an ocean. In this exciting coloring book, you will go for a tour of five ecosystems: woodland, marine, wetland, desert, and grassland. Each one provides a habitat—a place for creatures to live—where everything serves a purpose. For example, rocks and trees provide shade, and plants and water support life. When there is a good balance in an ecosystem, the residents of the habitat survive. But when there is not a good balance, the ecosystem is harmed, and survival is threatened. Polluted water leads to the death of fish and other animals, and the removal of trees threatens species as well.

Are you ready to join your tour guide, Mr. Turtle? He is waiting to show you the many wonderful places on our planet that are home to animals, big and small, and a variety of plants and flowers. So, get your crayons, colored pencils, and markers ready, and prepare to explore our planet's ecosystems!

Bibliographical Note

BOOST Exploring Ecosystems! An Environmentally Friendly Coloring Book, first published by Dover Publications, Inc., in 2013, is a revised edition of *Exploring Ecosystems! An Environmentally Friendly Coloring Book,* originally published by Dover in 2009.

International Standard Book Number

ISBN-13: 978-0-486-49405-0
ISBN-10: 0-486-49405-5

Manufactured in the United States by Courier Corporation
49405501   2013
www.doverpublications.com

Hey, everyone! Let's explore ecosystems!
Okay, Mr. Turtle. . . . But what exactly are ecosystems?

 RI.K.4 With prompting and support, ask and answer questions about unknown words in a text. Also **RI.K.7; RF.K.1.a, RF.K.1.c; L.K.6.**

An example of an ecosystem is the woodlands that we're hiking through. It is
made up of all of the animals, trees, plants, and land, as well as the climate.
All of these things work together to keep the ecosystem balanced.

 RI.K.2 With prompting and support, identify the main topic and retell key details of a text.
Also **RI.K.7; RF.K.1.b; SL.K.2; L.K.6.**

As trees grow, they produce seeds. The seeds
provide food for animals such as this squirrel.

 RI.K.1 With prompting and support, ask and answer questions about key details in a text.
Also **RI.K.2; RF.K.4.**

The ground below is also part of the ecosystem. Rabbits, moles, and some types of insects are just a few of the creatures that make their home underground.

 RI.K.7 With prompting and support, describe the relationship between illustrations and the text in which they appear. Also **RI.K.1; RF.K.1; SL.K.2; L.K.4.**

Deer eat the grass and use the tree cover as shade from the sun.

 RI.K.1 With prompting and support, ask and answer questions about key details in a text. Also **RI.K.10; RF.K.4.**

Late in the year, salmon leave the sea to lay their eggs in the rivers they were born in.
Some of the eggs become food for large animals such as this mother bear and her cubs.

CCSS **RI.K.3** With prompting and support, describe the connection between two individuals, events, ideas, or pieces of information in a text. Also **RI.K.2; RF.K.1; SL.K.2.**

Speaking of the sea, let's take a look at the marine ecosystem.

 RI.K.4 With prompting and support, ask and answer questions about unknown words in a text. Also **RI.K.7, RI.K.10; RF.K.4; L.K.6.**

Water covers most of our planet's surface.
There are many kinds of habitats, such as this coral reef.

This sea otter is eating an oyster while floating on top of an
underwater "forest" made from seaweed called *kelp*.

Under the sea, there is food for animals like this seal,
which is chasing a fish for its meal.

You can find a lot of sea creatures on the beach, too!

RI.K.1 With prompting and support, ask and answer questions about key details in a text.
Also **RI.K.10; RF.K.1.b, RF.K.4.**

Shhh. . . . This mother sea turtle has to come onto the land to lay her eggs,
but she spends the rest of her life in the ocean.

 CCSS **RI.K.2** With prompting and support, identify the main topic and retell key details of a text.
Also **RI.K.7; RF.K.1; SL.K.2.**

Let's go see some wetlands now.

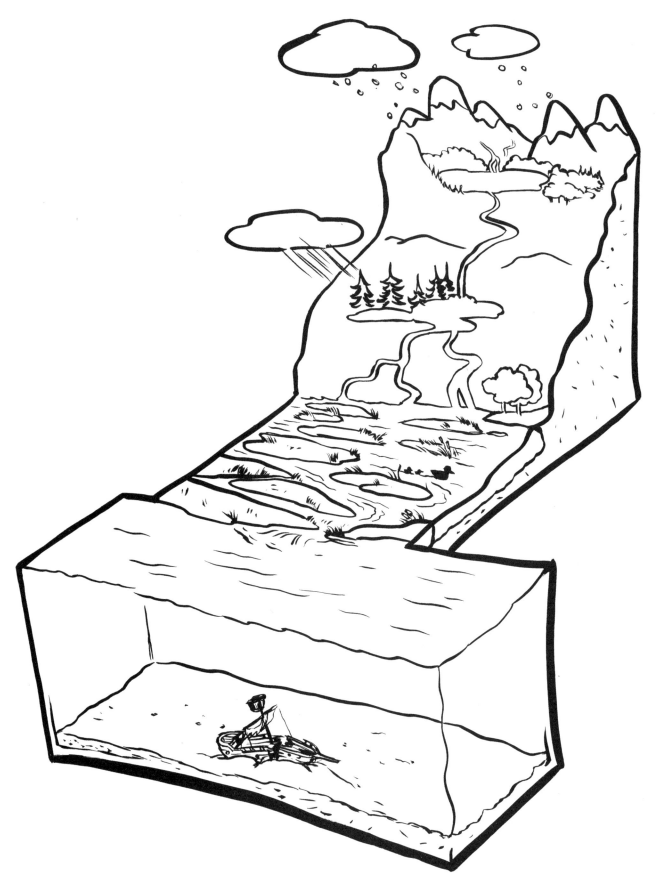

Water from rain and snow flows to the wetlands,
and the wetlands keep other areas from flooding.

Because there is so much water, lots of animals, like this beaver, live here.
The beaver helps the ecosystem by building a dam from wood and mud.

 RI.K.2 With prompting and support, identify the main topic and retell key details of a text.
Also **RI.K.1, RI.K.7; RF.K.4; L.K.6.**

Ducks live here, raising their ducklings in the safety of the wetlands.

 RI.K.10 Actively engage in group reading activities with purpose and understanding. Also **RI.K.7; RF.K.1.**

Even creatures as small as insects are part of the ecosystem, providing food for fish.

 RI.K.1 With prompting and support, ask and answer questions about key details in a text. Also **RI.K.10; RF.K.1.a, RF.K.1.c.**

And my favorite food, the crayfish, lives here, too!
Would you like a bite before we leave?
No, thank you, Mr. Turtle!

 RI.K.1 With prompting and support, ask and answer questions about key details in a text.
Also **RI.K.7; RF.K.1; L.K.4, L.K.6.**

Now we are at a desert, which is the opposite of wetlands.

Even though it's so dry, the desert is home to animals and plants,
which are part of the ecosystem and food chain.

 RI.K.7 With prompting and support, describe the relationship between illustrations and the text in which they appear. Also **RI.K.4; RF.K.4; SL.K.2; L.K.6.**

My old friend, the tortoise, loves this hot and dry climate!

 RI.K.10 Actively engage in group reading activities with purpose and understanding. Also **RI.K.7; RF.K.3.**

Bees are part of an ecosystem as they transfer pollen from cactus flowers.

 RI.K.4 With prompting and support, ask and answer questions about unknown words in a text. Also **RI.K.2, RI.K.7; RF.K.1.b; SL.K.2; L.K.6.**

Even though the desert looks vast to us, it may not offer enough space for many animals. Some of them—such as these longhorn sheep—even will compete for territory.

 RI.K.2 With prompting and support, identify the main topic and retell key details of a text. Also **RI.K.7; RF.K.4.**

This burrowing owl guards her babies in a cool underground nest
that once belonged to another creature.

 RI.K.7 With prompting and support, describe the relationship between illustrations and the text in which they appear. Also **RI.K.1; RF.K.3; SL.K.2.**

Let's go to the grasslands now, where it's not as hot.
Look at how these clouds provide shade!

 RI.K.10 Actively engage in group reading activities with purpose and understanding. Also
RI.K.7; RF.K.1; L.K.4.

This ecosystem is like the others we've seen, where animals and plants are part of the food chain. This bobcat is stalking his prey, a very fast jackrabbit.

 RI.K.7 With prompting and support, describe the relationship between illustrations and the text in which they appear. Also **RI.K.2; RF.K.4; L.K.4, L.K.6.**

Some animals are so big that they move at a slower pace.
These large buffalo take their time eating tons of grass each day.

 RI.K.1 With prompting and support, ask and answer questions about key details in a text. Also **RI.K.7; RF.K.1.b.**

Grasslands also are the perfect place for running free!

 RI.K.7 With prompting and support, describe the relationship between illustrations and the text in which they appear. Also **RI.K.10; RF.K.1; L.K.4, L.K.4.b.**

The grasslands are vast, but there still are plenty of tiny things living on the ground.

 RI.K.4 With prompting and support, ask and answer questions about unknown words in a text. Also **RI.K.1; L.K.1.e, L.K.6.**

Ecosystems are everywhere! Keep exploring!

 RI.K.10 Actively engage in group reading activities with purpose and understanding. Also **RF.K.4; SL.K.1.**